CiRCLES

by David A. Adler • illustrated by Edward Miller

Holiday House / New York

For Janet and Howard,
their children and grandchildren
—D. A. A.

To my mom
—E. M.

Text copyright © 2016 by David A. Adler
Illustrations copyright © 2016 by Edward Miller
All Rights Reserved
HOLIDAY HOUSE is registered in the U.S. Patent and Trademark Office.
Printed and Bound in April 2016 at Tien Wah Press, Johor Bahru, Johor, Malaysia.
The artwork was created digitally.
www.holidayhouse.com
First Edition
1 3 5 7 9 10 8 6 4 2

Library of Congress Cataloging-in-Publication Data

Names: Adler, David A., author. | Miller, Edward, 1964– illustrator.
Title: Circles / by David A. Adler ; illustrated by Edward Miller.
Description: First edition. | New York : Holiday House, [2016] | Audience:
Age 6–10. | Audience: K to grade 3.
Identifiers: LCCN 2015040848 | ISBN 9780823436422 (hardcover)
Subjects: LCSH: Circle—Juvenile literature. | Geometry—Juvenile literature.
Classification: LCC QA484 .A35 2016 | DDC 516/.152—dc23 LC record
available at http://lccn.loc.gov/2015040848

Visit www.davidaadler.com for more information on the author, for a list of his books and to download teacher's guides and educational materials. You can also learn more about the writing process, take fun quizzes and read select pages from David A. Adler's books.

Visit Edward Miller on Facebook at Edward Elementary.

A ball is round but it's not a **circle**. It's a **sphere**.

A sphere is a perfectly round three-dimensional object. All points on the outside of the sphere are the exact same distance to its center.

Basketballs and marbles are spheres.

3

Oranges and the Earth are approximate spheres. They are not perfectly round.

A can of peas is round but it's not a circle. It's a **cylinder**.

A cylinder is a three-dimensional object. It's a circular column. Cans, tubes and paper towel rolls are cylinders.

A pointy party hat is round but it's not a circle. It's a **cone**.

A cone is a three-dimensional object with a round base that gets narrower and narrower until it comes to a point.

Funnels, tepees and ice-cream cones are cones.

Ovals and **spirals** are also round but they're not circles.

This is a circle.

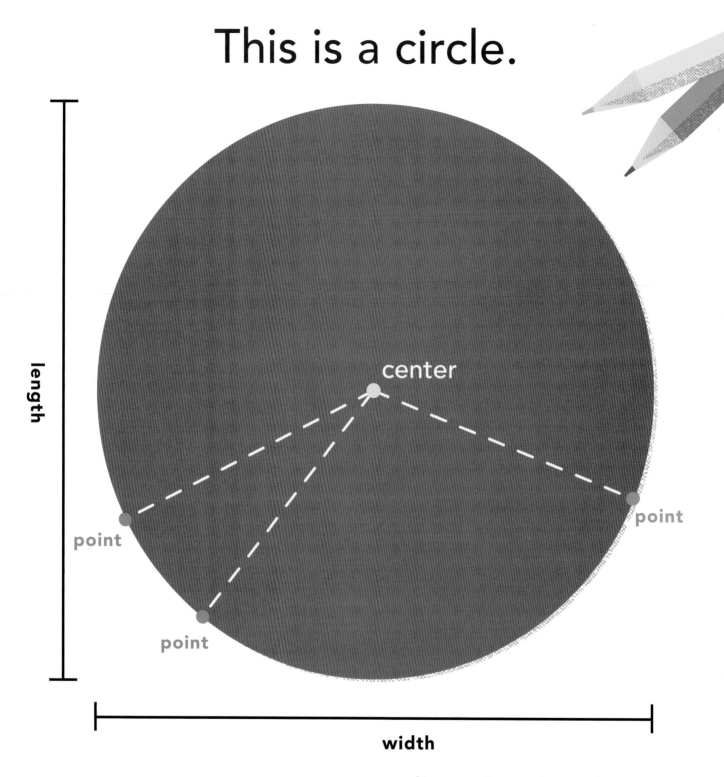

It is a closed round flat shape. It has **two dimensions**, **length** and **width**. All points on the outside edge of a circle are the exact same distance from its **center**.

With some ordinary school supplies you can learn about circles. You'll need a few sheets of paper, a pencil, a ruler, a pair of safe scissors and a small round dish.

Carefully turn the dish upside down and place it on a sheet of paper. Hold the dish in place with one hand. With the other hand, trace with a pencil around the rim of the dish. Take the dish away. You should have drawn a circle.

Now, with the scissors, carefully cut out the circle.

Carefully fold your paper circle in half. A circle is perfectly **symmetrical**. One half of the paper circle should exactly cover the other.

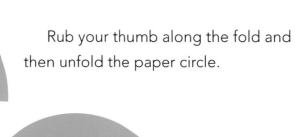

Rub your thumb along the fold and then unfold the paper circle.

You should see a straight crease that divides the paper circle in half.

Now do it again. Carefully fold your paper circle in half but not along the same line as before. Rub your thumb along the fold and then unfold the paper circle. You should see two straight creases.

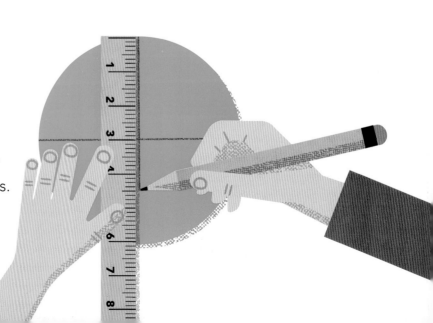

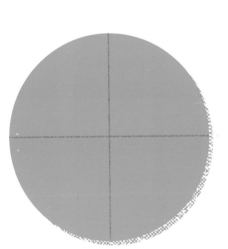

With the pencil and ruler draw two straight lines along the creases.

The point where the two lines **intersect** is the exact **center** of your paper circle.

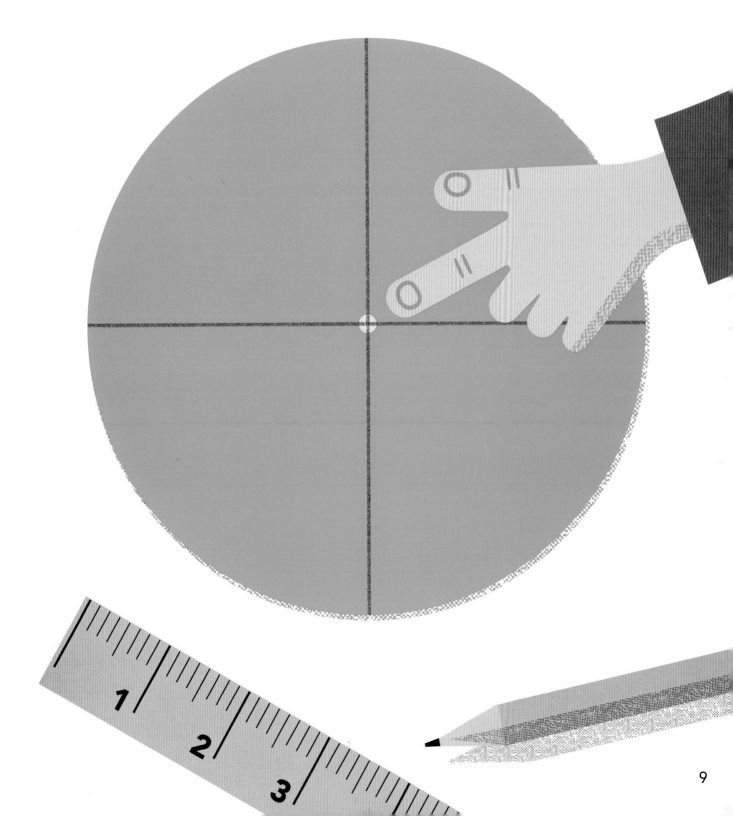

With the pencil and ruler, draw two more straight lines, each beginning at one edge of the circle, going through its center and ending at the other edge.

Measure all four lines.

They should all be the exact same length.

Each of those four lines, straight lines from one point on the outside edge through the circle's center to the opposite side, is called the circle's **diameter**.

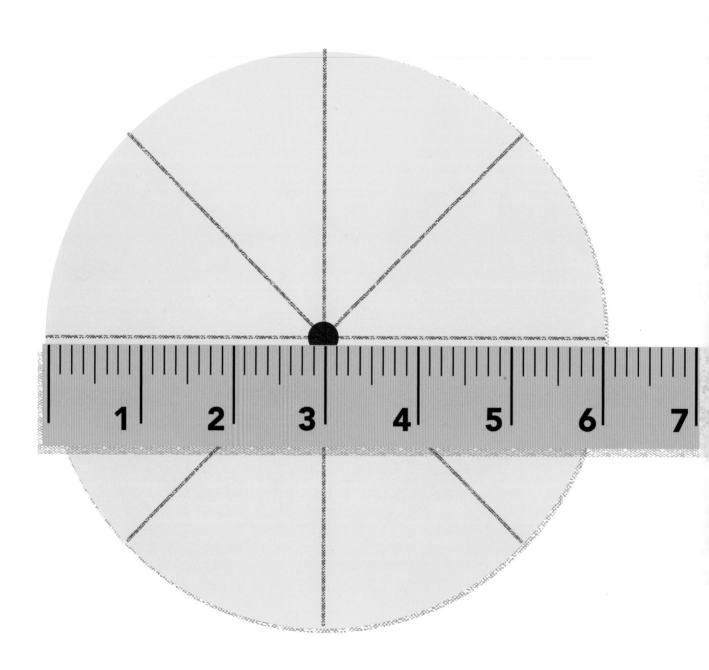

The diameter of a circle cuts the circle in half.
Each diameter of a circle is the same length as
any other diameter of that circle.

Now, with the ruler and pencil, draw a straight line from the outside edge to the circle's center.

That line is called the circle's **radius**.

Measure the radius.

A circle's radius is half the length of its diameter.

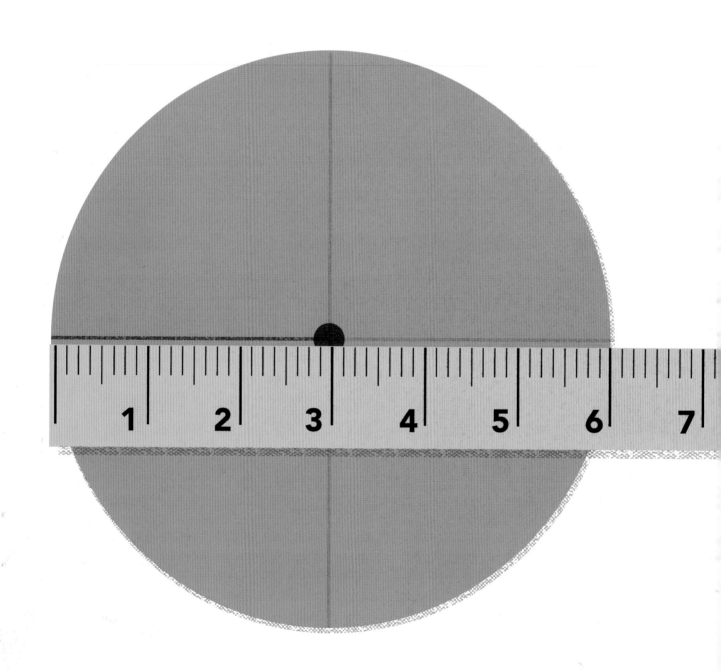

How many
radii do you
see?

Draw a second radius.

Look at the space between the two radii.

The radii cut the circle into two parts. Each is called a **sector** of the circle.

Unless the two radii are in a straight line, they cut the circle into two unequal parts.

The smaller is called a **minor sector**. The larger is called a **major sector**.

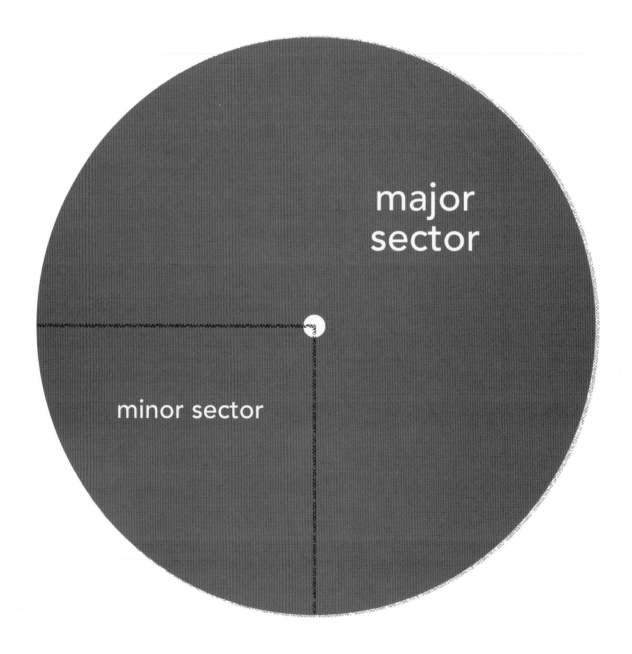

Which are the minor sectors?

Which are the major sectors?

15

With your ruler and pencil, draw a few more lines, each beginning at one point on the outside edge of the circle and going to another but not necessarily going through its center.

Each of those lines is called a **chord**.

A diameter is a chord. A radius is not a chord because only one of its ends is on the circle's outside edge.

Measure each chord.

The longest chord of any circle is its diameter.

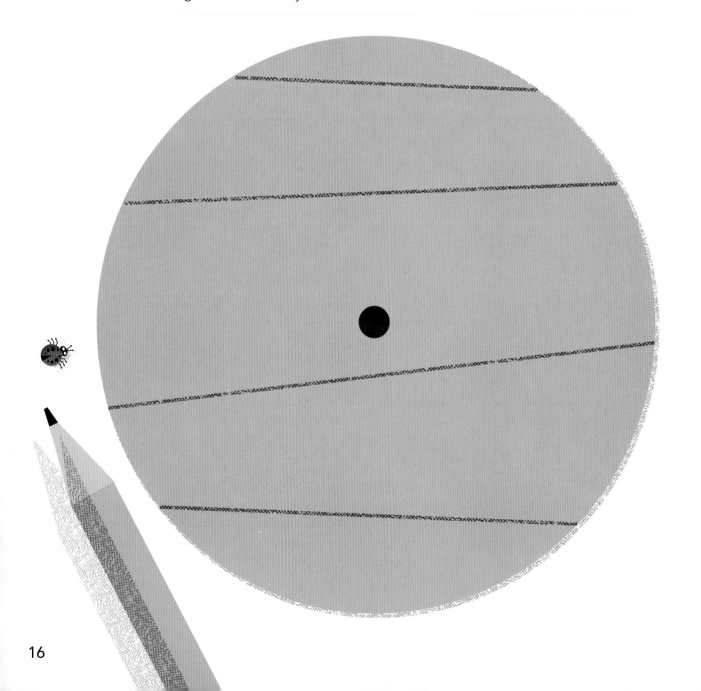

How many chords can you find?

A chord cuts a circle into two parts, two **segments**.

If the chord is a diameter, the two parts are equal in size.

If the chord is not a diameter, the parts are unequal. One part is bigger than the other. The smaller is called a **minor segment**. The larger is called a **major segment**.

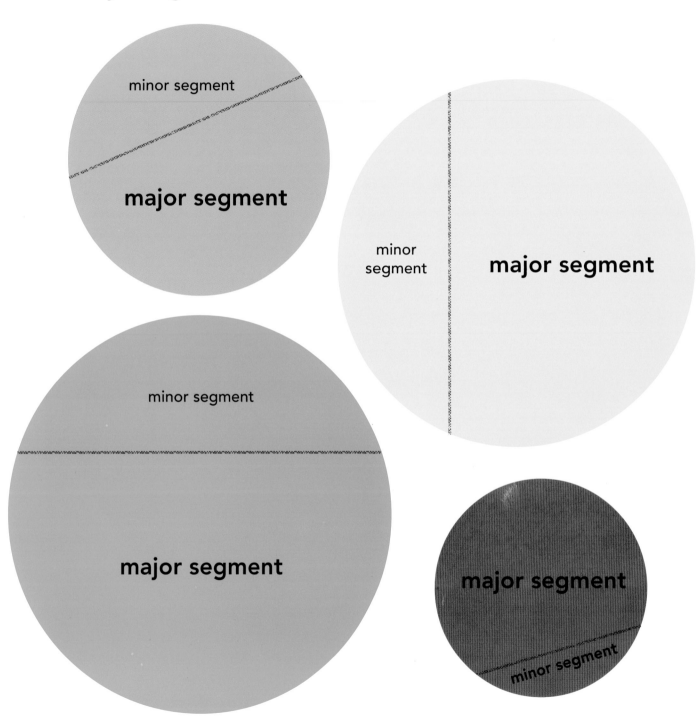

The line that forms the outside edge of a circle is called the circle's **circumference**.

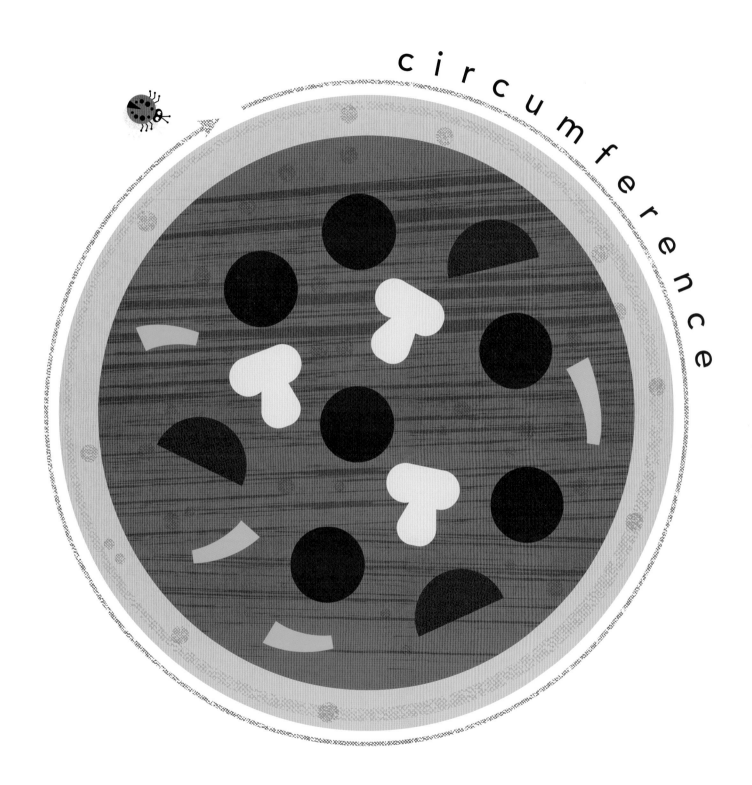

circumference

Each chord cuts the circumference of the circle into pieces. A piece of the circumference of a circle is called an **arc**.

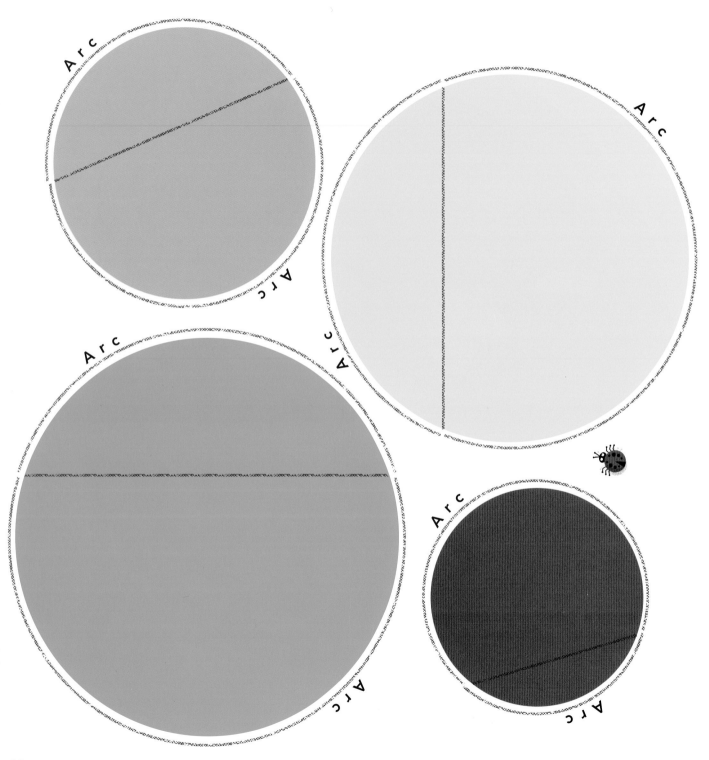

Again, carefully turn the dish upside down and place it on a sheet of paper. Hold the dish in place with one hand. With the other hand, trace with a pencil around the rim of the dish. Take the dish away. You should have drawn a circle.

Place the ruler so the straight edge of the ruler touches the circumference of the circle at just one point. With the pencil, draw that line. No matter how long you extend either endpoint of the line, it would touch the circle at just one point.

The line you drew is **tangent** to the circle.

Find the circumference of a circle.

With a can, a pencil, marker, ruler, safe scissors, calculator and sheet of paper you can learn how to find the circumference of a circle.

Stand the can up on the paper. With the pencil, trace around the rim of the can. Take the can off the paper and look at the circle you drew.

What's the length of the circumference of that circle?

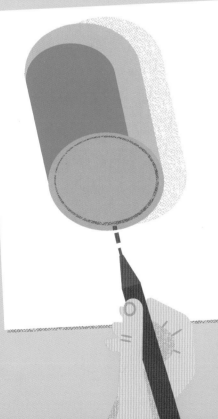

Make a small mark along the edge of the can.

Place the can on its side on the paper so the marked point of the can is directly on the paper. Mark that spot on the paper.

Now roll the can until the mark on the can is again directly on the paper. Mark that spot on the paper.

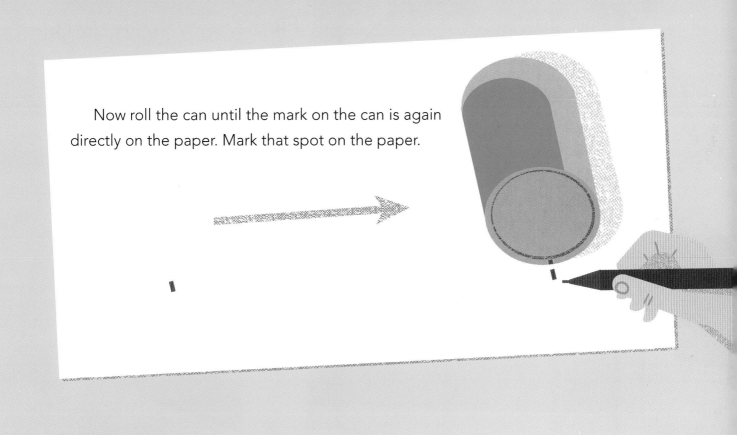

Now measure the distance between the two marks.
That distance is the circumference of the circle.

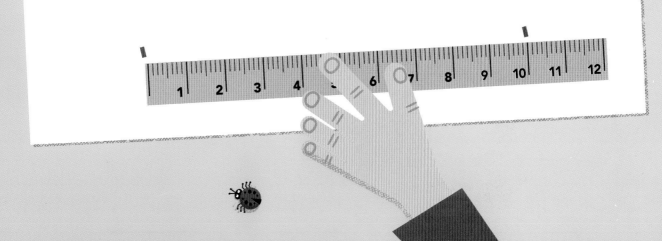

Find Pi (π).

With the scissors, carefully cut out the circle you drew by tracing around the can.

Carefully fold the paper circle in half so that one half of the paper circle exactly covers the other. Rub your thumb along the fold and then unfold the paper. That fold goes through the center of the circle. It's the circle's diameter.

Measure the diameter.

Now divide the circumference by the diameter. You may need a calculator for this.

Your answer should be approximately **3.14**.

No matter how small or large your circle, when you divide its circumference by its diameter, the answer is always slightly more than 3.14. That number is called **pi**, pronounced pie.

π is the symbol for pi.

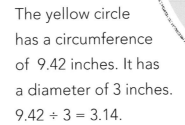

The yellow circle has a circumference of 9.42 inches. It has a diameter of 3 inches. 9.42 ÷ 3 = 3.14.

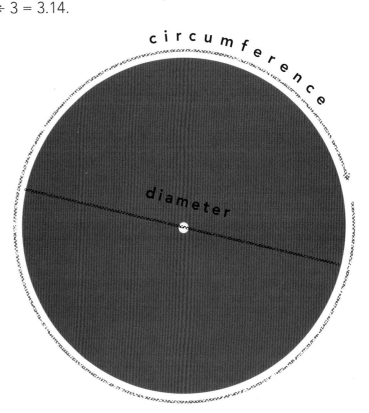

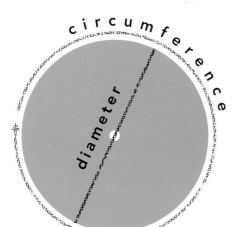

circumference ÷ diameter = π

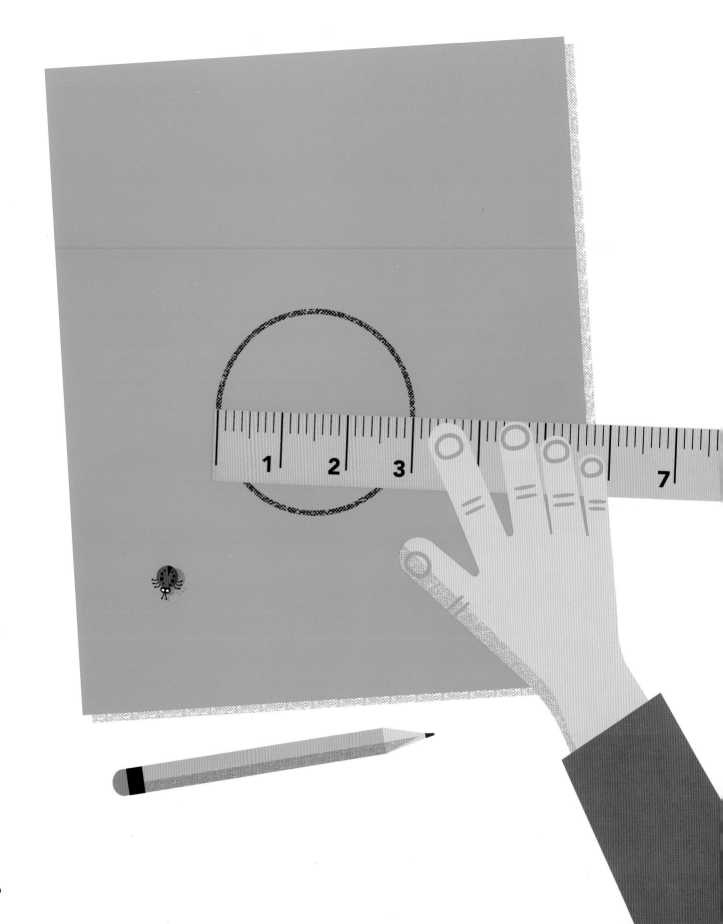

With a ruler, a tape measure, a sheet of paper, a pencil and another can you can prove this another way.

The top rim of the can is a circle. Stand the can up on the paper. With the pencil, trace around the rim of the can. Take the can off the paper and look at the circle you drew.

Slide the ruler over the circle. Find where the circle is widest. That's its diameter.

Wrap the tape measure around the rim of the can. The measure of the rim is its circumference.

The diameter of this can is 2 $^7/_8$". The circumference of the rim as measured with the tape is slightly more than 9" — about 9 $^1/_{32}$". 7/8 = .875 and 1/32 = .03125. Divide 9.03125 by 2.875 and you get 3.14.

Now that you know about pi you can find the circumference of a circle without measuring it. Simply multiply the length of the diameter by pi.

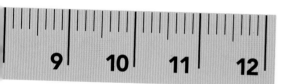

circumference ÷ diameter = π
or diameter x π = circumference

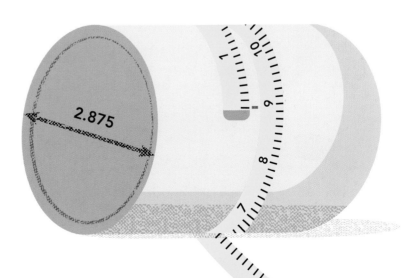

You can also use pi to find the **area**, the space inside a circle. Simply multiply the length of the radius by itself and multiply that by pi.

If the radius of a circle is 3 inches you would multiply 3 by 3 = 9. Then you multiply 9 by pi (3.14) and find that the area of the circle is 28.26 square inches. Now that you know about pi you can find the area of a circle without measuring it. Simply multiply the length of the radius by itself and multiply that by pi.

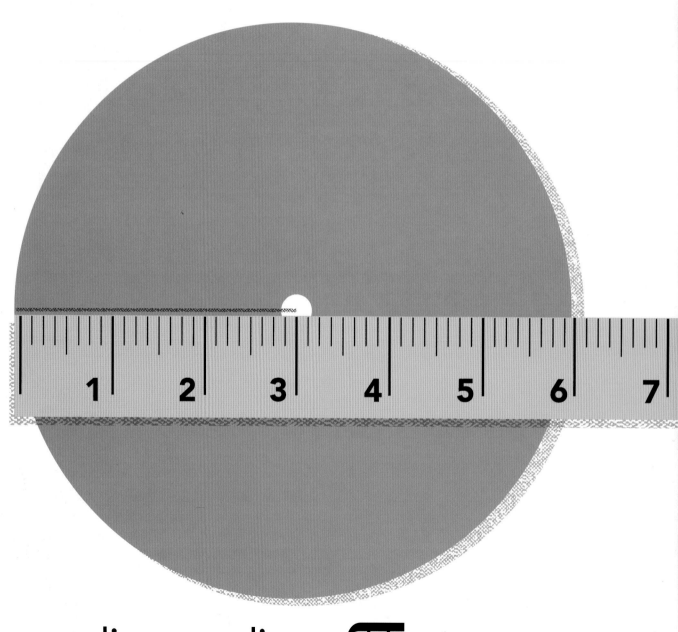

radius x radius x 𝛑 = area

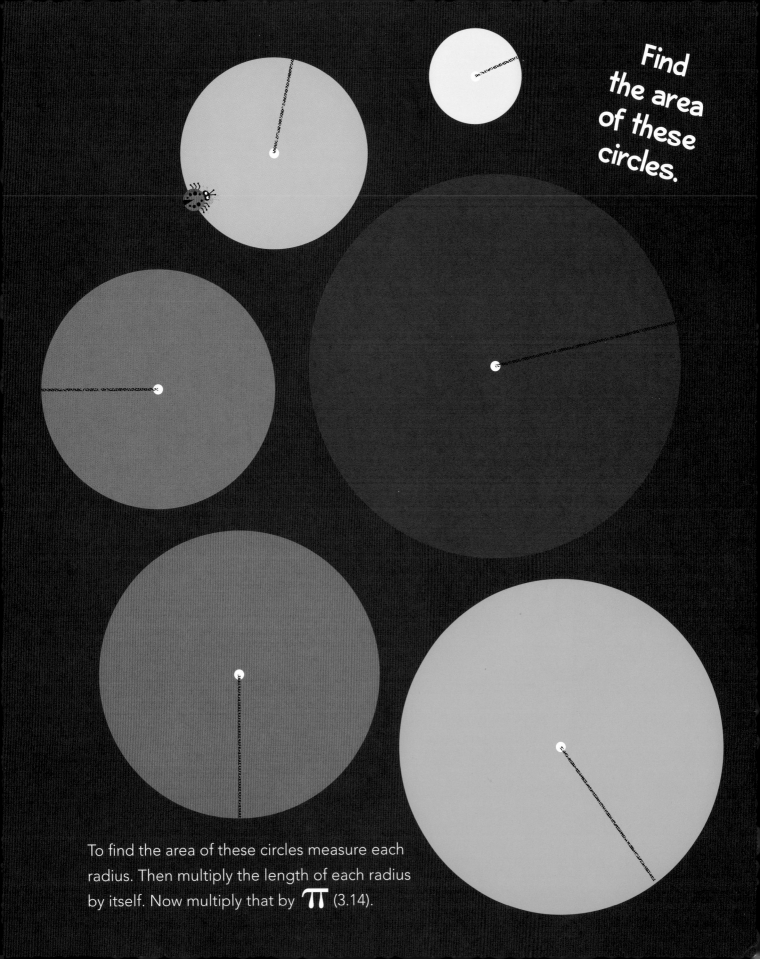

Find the area of these circles.

To find the area of these circles measure each radius. Then multiply the length of each radius by itself. Now multiply that by π (3.14).

The circle is a useful shape.

Wheels are circle-shaped. Just imagine if the wheels on your car or bicycle were square-shaped or triangle-shaped. You would have some very bumpy rides.

We use all sorts of machines, and machines need gears to make them work. Gears are circle-shaped. They're wheels with teeth.

There are lots of circles in nature. Many flowers, seeds, hats, buttons and bottle caps are circle-shaped.

Look in a mirror and there they are, the circle-shaped pupils of your eyes.

Ring-around-the-rosy is a circle game.

Rings, bracelets and necklaces are circle-shaped.

We live in a world of circles.

Glossary

Arc – any part of the outer edge, the circumference of a circle.

Chord – any straight line connecting two points on a circle.

Circle – a closed, round two-dimensional (flat) figure in which all points on the outer edge (or circumference) are the same distance to its center.

Circumference – a line that forms the outer edge of a circle or any two-dimensional (flat) figure.

Diameter – any straight line that begins at one point on the outer edge, the circumference, of a circle, goes through its center and ends at the circle's outer edge. It divides the circle exactly in half.

Pi (π) – a Greek letter used as the symbol for the constant value of the circumference of any circle when divided by its diameter. It is a very useful value. With it, if we know the diameter or radius of a circle we can find its circumference. If we know the radius of a circle, with it, we can find its area. The approximate value of pi is 3.14 or, as a fraction, 22/7.

Radii – more than one radius.

Radius – any straight line that goes from the center of a circle to its outer edge.

Sector – two radii of a circle and the arc between them form a sector, a section, of a circle. Unless the radii are in a straight line forming the diameter of the circle, they will form two sectors, one larger than the other. The larger sector is called a major sector. The smaller is called a minor sector.

Segment – a chord divides a circle into two parts of a circle. Each part is called a segment of the circle.

Sphere – a solid such as a ball in which all points on its outside are the same distance to its center.

Tangent – a straight line that touches a circle or any curved line at only one point.

Answers to Questions

Page 13: How many radii can you find? 9 radii

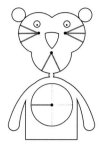

Page 15: Which are the minor sectors? Which are the major sectors?

Page 17: How many chords do you find? 20 chords

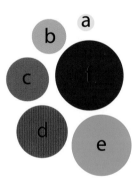

Page 29: Find the area of these circles.
a. .5 x 2 x 3.14 = 3.14
b. 1 x 2 x 3.14 = 6.28
c. 1.25 x 2 x 3.14 = 7.85
d. 1.5 x 2 x 3.14 = 9.42
e. 1.75 x 2 x 3.14 = 10.99
f. 2 x 2 x 3.14 = 12.56